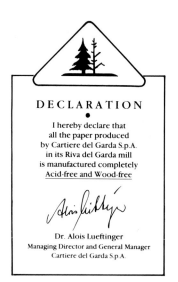

DECLARATION

I hereby declare that
all the paper produced
by Cartiere del Garda S.p.A.
in its Riva del Garda mill
is manufactured completely
<u>Acid-free and Wood-free</u>

Dr. Alois Lueftinger
Managing Director and General Manager
Cartiere del Garda S.p.A.

WOODLAND TREES

Written by
Theresa Greenaway

STECK-VAUGHN
L I B R A R Y
A Division of Steck-Vaughn Company

Austin, Texas

**Published in the United States in 1991
by Steck-Vaughn, Co., Austin, Texas,**
a subsidiary of National Education Corporation

A Templar Book
Devised and produced by The Templar Company plc
Pippbrook Mill, London Road, Dorking, Surrey RH4 1JE, Great Britain

Editor: Wendy Madgwick
Designer: Jane Hunt
Illustrators: Wendy and Clifford Meadway
American consultant: Helen Mageau, Frelinghuysen Arboretum, N.J.

Notes to Reader
There are some words in this book that are printed in **bold** type.
A brief explanation of these words is given in the glossary on p. 44.

All living things are given two Latin names when first classified by a
scientist. Some of them also have a common name, for example
white willow, *Salix alba*. In this book, the common name is used where
possible, but the scientific name is given when first mentioned.

Library of Congress Cataloging-in-Publication Data
Greenaway, Theresa, 1947-
Woodland trees / written by Theresa Greenaway.
p. cm. – (The Green World)
"A Templar Book" – T.p. verso.
Includes bibliographical references and index.
Summary: Describes different types of forests throughout the world and
the threats to their survival. Also discusses the importance of trees in
producing oxygen and the many products that we get from trees.
ISBN 0-8114-2732-3
1. Trees – Juvenile literature.   2. Forest flora – Juvenile literature.
3. Forests and forestry – Juvenile literature.
[1. Trees.   2. Forest plants.   3. Forests and forestry.]   I. Title.   II. Series.
QK475.8.G72   1991   90-37227
582.160909'52–dc20   CIP AC

Color separations by Positive Colour Ltd, Maldon, Essex, Great Britain
Printed and bound by L.E.G.O., Vicenza, Italy
1 2 3 4 5 6 7 8 9 0 LE 95 94 93 92 91

Photographic credits
t = top, b = bottom, l = left, r = right
Cover: Bruce Coleman; page 9 RIDA/David Bayliss;
page 10 Bruce Coleman/Eric Crichton; page 11 Bruce Coleman/Hans
Reinhard; page 13 Bruce Coleman/Hans Reinhard; page 14 Bruce
Coleman/John Shaw; page 17 Bruce Coleman/Eric Crichton;
page 21 Bruce Coleman/Hans Reinhard; page 22 Bruce Coleman/
J. Grande; page 27 Bruce Coleman/Hans Reinhard; Frank Lane/
Holt Studios; page 29*t* Frank Lane/Holt Studios; page 29*b* Forestry
Commission; page 30 Bruce Coleman/D. and J. Bartlett;
page 36 Forestry Commission; page 37 Forestry Commission; page 38 Bruce
Coleman/M. Timothy O'Keefe; page 39 Bruce Coleman/
Fritz Prenzel; page 40 Frank Lane/R.P. Lawrence; page 41
Frank Lane/Holt Studios; page 42 Bruce Coleman/S. Kaufman;
page 43 Bruce Coleman/J. Anthony.

CONTENTS

GREEN WORLD

This tree shows the different groups of plants that are found in the world. It does not show how they developed or their relationship with each other.

PALM TREES

MONOCOTYLEDONS

BROAD-LEAVED TREES

DICOTYLEDONS

CONIFEROUS (OR FIR) TREES (Gymnosperms)

FLOWERING PLANTS (Angiosperms)

SMALL PLANTS

FERNS, CLUBMOSSES, AND HORSETAILS (Pteridophytes)

MOSSES AND LIVERWORTS (Bryophytes)

ALGAE

GREEN PLANTS

ANIMALS

PLANTS

FUNGI AND LICHENS

BACTERIA

SLIME MOLDS

LIVING THINGS

Group 1
Magnolias and tulip trees
■ These have many primitive features
■ Their floral parts are spirally arranged
■ The leaves are often leathery

Group 2
Oaks, beeches, elms, walnuts, chestnuts, birches, planes, alders, hornbeams, and hickories
■ Includes almost all of the important temperate timber trees
■ They are mostly wind-pollinated, with tiny greenish flowers arranged in catkins

Group 3
Apples, pears, plums, cherries, thorns, horse chestnuts, buckeyes, maples, and hollies
■ Insect-pollinated trees with conspicuous, usually white or colored, flowers
■ The leaves are often lobed or compound

Group 4
Willows, poplars, and lindens
■ Leaves simple, some with shallow lobes
■ Flowers whitish or greenish, wind- or insect-pollinated

Group 5
Ashes
■ Wind- or insect-pollinated, with winged, one-seeded fruits
■ The leaves are pinnate

The land area of the world is divided into ten main zones depending on the plants that grow there. Broad-leaved woodland trees are found in temperate parts of the world.

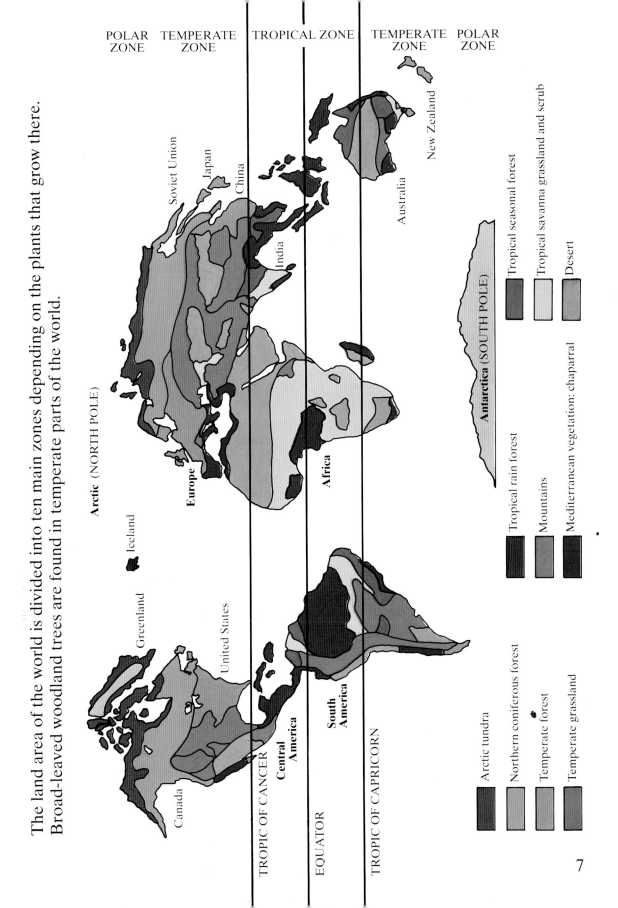

POLAR ZONE   TEMPERATE ZONE   TROPICAL ZONE   TEMPERATE ZONE   POLAR ZONE

Arctic (NORTH POLE)

Soviet Union
Japan
China
India
Europe
Africa
Iceland
Greenland
United States
Canada
Central America
South America
New Zealand
Australia
Antarctica (SOUTH POLE)

TROPIC OF CANCER
EQUATOR
TROPIC OF CAPRICORN

Arctic tundra
Northern coniferous forest
Temperate forest
Temperate grassland

Tropical rain forest
Mountains
Mediterranean vegetation: chaparral

Tropical seasonal forest
Tropical savanna grassland and scrub
Desert

WOODLAND TREES

A woodland or broad-leaved tree is a tall plant with a single woody stem, or **trunk**, and a **crown** of leafy branches. Broad-leaved trees are flowering plants or angiosperms (see p. 24).

Trees can live a long time. It is not unusual for them to live 200 to 300 years, and oaks (*Quercus* species) may live for even longer. Bushes are also woody plants, but these have a number of woody stems and grow into fairly low, twiggy shrubs.

Trees have leaves that contain the green pigment **chlorophyll**. This uses the energy in sunlight to convert water and carbon dioxide gas into sugars in a process called **photosynthesis**. The gas oxygen, which is needed by almost all living things, is also produced.

A tree grows taller from the tips of its twigs, and the tree trunk grows a little thicker each year. This growth can be seen as annual rings when a tree is cut down. The age of the tree can be found by counting these rings.

Types of trees

The leaves of broad-leaved trees are flat, wide, and usually quite thin. They are very different from the hard, narrow needles of conifer trees such as pine, fir, and spruce. Most broad-leaved trees are deciduous, that is, their leaves fall in the autumn, leaving the twigs bare throughout winter. There are exceptions to this, as hollies, laurels, and some magnolias and oaks are evergreen. Their leaves are tough and leathery, so they are not damaged by frost and cold winds in the winter.

Red oak
(*Quercus rubra*)

American sycamore
(*Platanus occidentalis*)

European beech
(*Fagus sylvatica*)

European ash
(*Fraxinus excelsior*)

The earliest broad-leaved trees

The first flowering plants were small trees and bushes. Some of these had leaves and flowers very similar to living magnolias (*Magnolia* species). Fossils of leaves resembling modern birches (*Betula* species), planes (*Platanus* species), poplars (*Populus* species), and the katsura tree (*Cercidiphyllum japonicum*) have also been found. These early angiosperm fossils come from Lower Cretaceous rocks in the U.S., Canada, Greenland, Europe, and Asia. They are between 100 and 141 million years old.

poplar

birch

plane

Laurel
(*Laurus nobilis*)

Holly
(*Ilex aquilifolium*)

■ Woodland or broad-leaved trees are flowering plants or angiosperms.
■ They all have trunks, roots, and a crown of stems and leaves.
■ Their leaves are usually flat, wide, and thin.
■ They are green-leaved plants and contain the green pigment chlorophyll. They make their food by combining carbon dioxide gas and water to make sugar using the energy from sunlight.
■ Some broad-leaved trees are deciduous, losing their leaves at the end of the growing season, while others are evergreen, losing only a few leaves throughout the year.

THE TEMPERATE FOREST

Temperate forest is one of the world's large natural types of vegetation, called a **zone** (see map on p. 7). A zone, together with the animals that live in it, is known as a **biome**. About 15 percent of the Earth's surface is temperate forest – woods where deciduous, broad-leaved trees grow. However, because of its fertile brown soil, mild climate, and many streams and rivers, large areas of what were once woods are now towns, farms, or industrial estates.

The largest temperate forests are in the northern hemisphere, in the eastern U.S., the U.K., west and central Europe, and eastern Asia. The climate is mild, with temperatures falling to about 32°F in winter and rising to about 70°F in summer. Winters are neither as long nor as dark as those suffered by the taiga – the coniferous forests of the north. There is no dry season, and between 20 and 60 inches of rain fall throughout the year.

Temperate rain forests
There is far less land in the temperate regions of the southern hemisphere. Smaller areas of temperate forests are found in southern Chile, Tasmania, and New Zealand. There the southern beeches (*Nothofagus* species) prevail. The climate is much wetter, and the luxuriant growth of mixed broad-leaved and conifer trees are often called temperate rain forests.

The importance of all the world's forests is very great. They provide a home for numerous creatures – birds, insects, mammals, and many kinds of plants and fungi such as mushrooms and toadstools. They also help to control the world's weather patterns and to keep the amounts of oxygen and carbon dioxide in the air constant (see p. 37).

Northern forests

The dominant, or most abundant, trees of the northern forests are species of oaks, chestnuts, maples, hickories, ashes, lindens, and beeches.

Deciduous forests

A mature, deciduous forest is a three-tiered **ecosystem** (the plants and animals in an area). The top tier or layer is the **canopy**, made up of the crowns of the tallest trees. Below this is the **understory** with smaller trees and bushes. The third layer is the forest floor, where seedling trees, small flowering plants, ferns, and mosses grow.

Each layer provides a different kind of habitat and so is suitable for different animals, birds, and insects. Each of these layers can be divided further into smaller "micro-habitats" – a rotting log, the tree trunk, a grassy clearing – so it is clear that the forest is a very complex system indeed.

As most broad-leaved trees lose their leaves in autumn, the forest in early spring and winter has a very different appearance than it has in the summer. The leafless canopy is open, allowing sunlight through to the ground.

forest canopy

under - story

forest floor

EUROPE'S WOODLAND TREES

Europe once had a far greater variety of trees in its woods, but during the Pleistocene epoch, which began 2,500,000 years ago, successive ice ages swept over the land. The ice killed the plants and trees. Also, the land near the ice sheet was treeless, rather like the Arctic tundra today, with only a few hardy plants able to survive.

When warmer weather returned, surviving trees slowly grew and reproduced to form new forests.

However, many trees had died out and failed to return, including tulip trees (*Liriodendron* species) and wing-nut trees (*Pterocarya* species). The surviving species made up the forests that covered most of Europe until they were chopped down. Germany has mixed forests of beech and silver fir (*Abies alba*), a conifer. France has groves of lindens (*Tilia* species), poplars, and chestnuts (*Castanea* species), and most of the U.K. was once covered with oaks.

**English or Pedunculate Oak
(*Quercus robur*)**
Found in Europe, Russia, North Africa, and southwest Asia, this is the wood that mighty galleons (ships) were made from. About 100 feet tall, it can live up to 800 years.

**European Beech
(*Fagus sylvatica*)**
The dense crown of this 100-foot-tall tree casts a deep shade. Beechwoods grow in parts of southern England and are widespread in Europe. The fruits contain small, edible nuts.

**Sweet Chestnut
(*Castanea sativa*)**
A tree of southern Europe that now grows as far north as southern England. It is famous for its large, edible seed – inside a very prickly fruit! It grows up to about 100 feet tall.

The sycamore maple

The Romans brought the sycamore maple (*Acer pseudoplatanus*) to Britain. It grows very easily and is quite a problem in southern England, where its vigorous seedlings spring up in gardens and woodland alike. It is hardy enough to grow well even in exposed places in the colder north and Scotland. Although not widely planted in the U.S., it is also a problem tree in America.

European Ash
(*Fraxinus excelsior*)
Identified in winter by its large, black buds, this ash grows to about 130 feet. It is one of the last trees to open its leaves in spring. Each fruit has one seed which is winged.

Aspen
(*Populus tremula*)
Aspens are the first trees to grow along woodland margins. They spread by suckers as well as seeds. Long-stalked leaves tremble in the slightest breeze. It grows to 50 feet.

Large-leaved Linden
(*Tilia platyphyllos*)
Common in many European woodlands, this 130-foot-tall tree is often planted along roadsides and in parks. Bees love the scented, nectar-rich flowers.

NORTH AMERICAN TREES

The deciduous woodlands of North America cover the eastern states of the U.S., reaching north into Canada and south to the warm, subtropical vegetation of Florida. These are valuable woods, because they contain so many kinds of temperate broad-leaved trees. These forests can roughly be divided into four areas. Widespread and common in all of these are the sugar and red maple (*Acer saccharum* and *A. rubrum*) and the basswood (*Tilia americana*) (see map below).

Autumn beauty

It is only possible here to give a glimpse of the richness of these woodlands. In autumn, the colors of the dying leaves are spectacular – the reds of the oaks, the flame colors of the maples, and the yellows of the birch and the tulip trees.

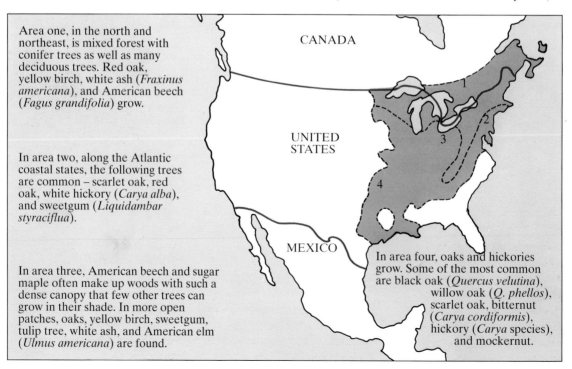

Area one, in the north and northeast, is mixed forest with conifer trees as well as many deciduous trees. Red oak, yellow birch, white ash (*Fraxinus americana*), and American beech (*Fagus grandifolia*) grow.

In area two, along the Atlantic coastal states, the following trees are common – scarlet oak, red oak, white hickory (*Carya alba*), and sweetgum (*Liquidambar styraciflua*).

In area three, American beech and sugar maple often make up woods with such a dense canopy that few other trees can grow in their shade. In more open patches, oaks, yellow birch, sweetgum, tulip tree, white ash, and American elm (*Ulmus americana*) are found.

In area four, oaks and hickories grow. Some of the most common are black oak (*Quercus velutina*), willow oak (*Q. phellos*), scarlet oak, bitternut (*Carya cordiformis*), hickory (*Carya* species), and mockernut.

CANADA

UNITED STATES

MEXICO

Scarlet Oak
(*Quercus coccinea*)

The tall, narrow crown of this 80-foot tree bears deeply lobed leaves. The acorns are less than an inch long and take two years to ripen. It is often planted in parks and gardens.

Western Balsam Poplar
(*Populus trichocarpa*)

A fast-growing 200-foot-tall tree of western North America, this poplar has sticky, strongly scented buds. Flowers are borne in catkins, and tiny fruits release masses of fluffy seeds.

Yellow Birch
(*Betula lutea*)

One of the largest birches, reaching 100 feet, this tree grows in eastern Canada and the northeast U.S. The bark is yellowish and the young shoots have a pleasant smell.

Basswood
(*Tilia americana*)

Like other lindens, the white flowers are a good source of nectar for bees. It grows to 100 feet and has a narrow crown. The heart-shaped leaves are about 8 inches long.

Mockernut
(*Carya tomentosa*)

A common hickory of the eastern forests, this 100-foot tree has large leaves that have a sweet smell. The fruit has a very hard shell with a small, edible nut.

Sugar Maple
(*Acer saccharum*)

This 120-foot maple has brilliantly colored autumn leaves. Its sweet sap can be made into maple syrup. Winged fruits help to spread the seeds.

WOODLAND TREES OF ASIA

Many of the same groups of trees of the western woodlands are also found in northeast Asia and Japan. There are oaks, beeches, chestnuts, birches, alder, maples, and lindens. Some, like the Japanese elm (*Ulmus japonica*), grow in large forests. Others, such as the katsura tree and the pagoda tree, are found only in Asian woods.

In Japan and China, cherry trees have been grown for their beautiful flowers for hundreds of years. The original parents of some of these trees have been forgotten, but most of the ornamental flowering cherries have descended from the Japanese cherry (*Prunus serratula*). It is probably not a Japanese tree at all, but came first from China. It is now very rare, but there are many different types or **cultivars**.

Other kinds of Japanese cherries have been bred to produce lovely trees like the Yoshino cherry (*P. yedoensis*). The white blossoms open before the leaves and cover the whole crown. It is very popular in Japan, Europe, and the U.S. and is often planted in parks and gardens.

Katsura Tree
(*Cercidiphyllum japonicum*)
Found in China and Japan, this valuable timber tree grows to over 100 feet. The nearly round leaves turn bright yellow in autumn. Male and female flowers are on separate trees.

White Mulberry
(*Morus alba*)
This small, 30-foot tree is the foodplant of the silkworm. Its native home is China, but it is cultivated widely in Asia. The female flowers ripen into deep-pink fruit.

Japanese Maple
(*Acer japonicum*)
In Japan, China, and Korea, this maple grows to 50 feet, but many very much smaller cultivars are planted in gardens all over the world. The leaves have seven to eleven lobes.

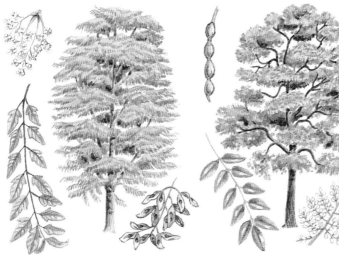
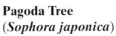

Tree of Heaven
(*Ailanthus altissima*)
This 100-foot Chinese tree also thrives in the west, even in cities. Its compound leaves can be 3 feet long! Female trees produce large clusters of winged fruits.

Pagoda Tree
(*Sophora japonica*)
Native to China and Korea, this 80-foot tree has twisted branches. It was once planted in Chinese cemeteries and temple courtyards. The white flowers are in large spires.

Japanese Big-leaved Magnolia
(*Magnolia hypoleuca*)
An 80-foot-tall tree with large, broad leaves, this magnolia has lovely cream flowers with a strong scent. The red, conelike fruit is 6 inches long, with bright orange seeds.

Ornamental cherries
Japan is famous for its many varieties of flowering cherry trees. Wild cherry trees grow naturally along the edges of woodlands. They like plenty of light, so although they grow quite tall, eventually larger forest trees grow above them.

TREES OF THE SOUTH

Southern Chile, Tasmania, and most of New Zealand are naturally covered with thick forests of mixed broad-leaved and conifer trees. The broad-leaved trees are almost all species of one group – the southern beeches.

The forests of Chile change from tall trees in the north to windswept, stunted bushes at the extreme southerly tip (see map). The roblé grows the farthest north. Roblé and coigue once covered vast areas of the foothills of the Andes, but many have been felled for their valuable timber. The raoul (*Nothofagus procera*) also grows in these forests.

On slopes between 4,000 and 5,000 feet, the Antarctic beech and lenga grow. These are sometimes in mixed forests with the monkey puzzle, a conifer.

Farther south, into Patagonia and Tierra del Fuego, there are forests of Antarctic beech, lenga, and oval-leaved southern beech. In very exposed places, where the soil is often thin, these trees are no more than bushes.

The southern beech forests of Chile
From Santiago down the coastal strip and slopes of the Andes to Tierra del Fuego are some of the finest beech woods. Southern beeches bear female and male flowers in separate clusters.

Roblé
(*Nothofagus obliqua*)

Coigue
(*Nothofagus dombeyi*)

Antarctic beech
(*Nothofagus antarctica*)
together with lenga
(*Nothofagus pumilio*)

Oval-leaved
southern beech
(*Nothofagus betuloides*)

Santiago

CHILE

ARGENTINA

Tierra del
Fuego

Antarctic Beech
(*Nothofagus antarctica*)
A deciduous tree found on the southernmost Andean slopes and islands. It can reach 100 feet in height, but in exposed places it is much shorter.

Coigue
(*Nothofagus dombeyi*)
This is a 80-foot-tall evergreen tree whose small glossy leaves are speckled with darker spots. There is an orange-colored layer beneath the bark.

New Zealand Red Beech
(*Nothofagus fusca*)
Large forests of this fine 100-foot-tall tree grow in the wetter parts of New Zealand. The leaves turn bright colors before falling in autumn.

Kowhai
(*Sophora tetraptera*)
The national flower of New Zealand, the kowhai is a small tree only 30 feet tall. It has evergreen, ferny leaves and clusters of yellow flowers.

Roblé Beech
(*Nothofagus obliqua*)
A 100-foot-tall, deciduous tree, it has dark leaves that look as if they have been pleated. Like other southern beeches, the flowers and fruits are tiny.

Tasmanian Beech
(*Nothofagus cunninghamii*)
A huge, 200-foot-tall tree that forms dense forests across western Tasmania. It is an evergreen, with useful, pink-colored timber.

19

ROOTS, TRUNK, AND CROWN

The young tree seedling pushes its first root straight down into the soil. As the tree grows, side roots grow out from it. Like twigs, roots can only lengthen at their tips. In deep soil, some roots grow downward, while others spread out, reaching great distances away from the tree.

Older roots are thick, tough, and woody. At the tips of the youngest, tiniest rootlets there are minute root hairs. These absorb water and dissolved nutrients (food substances) from the soil.

When a tree is felled, the different layers in the trunk can be seen clearly. The outer layer is the **bark**. It protects the living layer of wood beneath. The **phloem**, immediately beneath the bark, conducts the **sap**, made up of sugar and water, from the leaves to the rest of the tree. The next layer is the **cambium**, which is only one cell thick. It is the growing layer, gradually making the tree trunk and branches thicker, year by year. Inside the cambium is the **sapwood**, made up of **xylem** cells that conduct water and minerals from the tiniest roots to the outermost twigs and leaves. The central core of the trunk is called the **heartwood**. It contains chemicals called tannins that prevent attack from insects and mold.

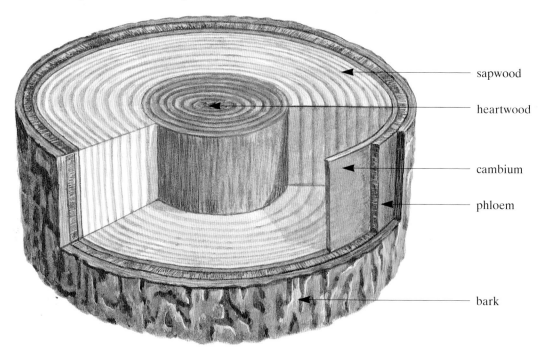

sapwood

heartwood

cambium

phloem

bark

The crown

The crown of broad-leaved trees is spreading and rounded. The unevenly spaced branches are very twiggy, supporting the leaves so that sunlight can fall upon them. Twigs, branches, and trunks have to be flexible enough to sway in the wind without snapping, and strong enough to bear the leaves and often heavy crops of large fruits such as walnuts, acorns, horse chestnuts, or crab apples.

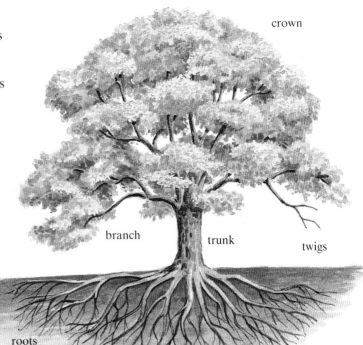

crown

branch

trunk

twigs

roots

Suckers

Many poplar trees send up **suckers**. These are shoots that grow from the tree's roots, forming a thicket around the tree. If the tree blows down, the tallest sucker grows up to replace it. Elms can also spread by means of suckers.

Thorns

Hawthorns (*Crataegus*), blackthorn (*Prunus spinosa*), common pear (*Pyrus communis*), and black locust (*Robinia pseudacacia*) have very sharp thorns, especially on their lower branches. These protect the tree from browsing animals.

21

LEAVES

The leaves of woodland trees, like all green plants, contain chlorophyll. Chlorophyll uses the energy in sunlight to convert carbon dioxide, a gas in the air, and water, taken from the soil by the roots, into sugars. These sugars are then changed into fats, starches, and cellulose and stored. Oxygen made during photosynthesis passes out into the air.

The skin or **cuticle** of the leaf is waterproof. Tiny holes, called **stomata**, are scattered over the leaf's surface, mainly on the underside. These allow the gases oxygen, carbon dioxide, and water vapor to enter and leave the leaf. On a warm day, water vapor on the surface of the leaf evaporates or dries, thus cooling the leaf. If too much water is lost, the leaf wilts. To prevent this from happening, the stomata close during the hottest part of the day.

Why do trees shed their leaves in autumn? Unlike evergreen conifer forests of the cold north or mountain slopes, broad-leaved trees grow in regions with less severe winters and longer summers. In the summer, their leaves produce enough sugars for the tree to grow, flower, fruit, form next year's buds, and survive the winter. The thin leaves would be damaged in wintry weather, so they are shed.

Evergreen broad-leaved trees
These have thick, waxy cuticles, just like conifer leaves. Some oaks are evergreen, as are some southern beeches. Hollies are well known for their spiny evergreen leaves and their red berries. Their tough leaves are very resistant to wind, frost, and snow. Leaves at the top of holly trees, out of reach of browsing animals, are not at all spiny.

Autumn colors

Besides the green chlorophyll, there are other colored pigments in the leaf. These are usually hidden by the chlorophyll. During autumn, the chlorophyll is broken down, as are the other pigments. Some minerals are reabsorbed by the tree. Waste products pass into the dying leaf for disposal. As all these complicated chemical changes take place, the leaves change color. In northeast North America, the trees give the best autumn display. There maples and oaks turn yellow, orange, scarlet, crimson, purple, and brown (see p. 14).

European ash
(*Fraxinus excelsior*)
simply turns yellowish-green

aspens
(*Populus*
species) turn
clear yellow

horse chestnut (*Aesculus hippocastanum*) and pedunculate oak turn orange-brown

All Shapes and Sizes

Woodland trees show a great variety of leaf shapes. Simple leaves have a leaf blade, and a stalk, or petiole. The blade of lobed leaves has fingerlike projections, and compound leaves have a stalk with several leaflets attached to it.

common or European beech

oriental beech
(*Fagus orientalis*)

stag's horn sumach
(*Rhus typhina*)

white ash
(*Fraxinus americana*)

American oak

scarlet oak

sycamore maple
(*Acer pseudoplatanus*)

Japanese
maple

silver maple
(*Acer saccharinum*)

white willow (*Salix alba*)

raoul

FLOWERS, FRUITS, AND SEEDS

Flowers are the reproductive parts of an angiosperm that produce the male and female sex cells. The flowers have petals that surround the male **stamens** and female **carpels**. When **pollen** from the stamens lands on the female part of a flower it is called **pollination**. The male cell in the pollen fuses with or **fertilizes** the female **ovule**. These grow into a seed, safe within the **fruit**.

The flowers of broad-leaved trees are pollinated either by wind or by insects. Wind-pollinated flowers are often clustered along a hanging stem, forming a catkin. Insect-pollinated flowers attract pollinators with sweet scents, sugary nectar, and sometimes bright petals. Their pollen is sticky and clings to the insects' bodies.

The fertilized ovule develops into a fruit that contains one or more seeds. Fast-growing trees, such as hazels (*Corylus avellana*), birches, and poplars begin to flower and fruit within 10 to 15 years. The taller, long-lived trees such as oaks and beeches do not begin to flower until they are much older, and may produce fertile seeds only once every few years.

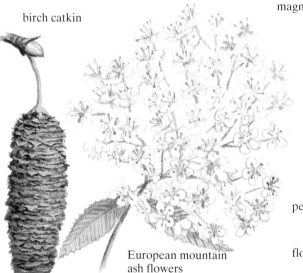

birch catkin

European mountain ash flowers

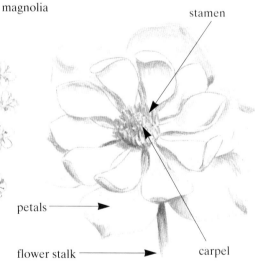

magnolia

stamen

petals

flower stalk

carpel

Wind or insect pollination?
Wind-pollinated flowers only have the tiny remains of greenish petals, and usually open early in spring before the leaves. The powdery pollen is released in large amounts. Trees with catkins include oaks, birches, and hazels.

Maples and lindens have greenish flowers that attract thousands of bees and other insects with their nectar. Flowers with large petals, or small-petaled flowers grouped in flowerheads, include horse chestnuts, European mountain ashes, hawthorns, elders, and magnolias.

Seed Dispersal

The seeds of angiosperms are enclosed in a fruit. The fruits of many trees such as maples and ashes have a papery wing. When they fall, they are carried away from the parent tree by the wind. Birches and alders have light, winged seeds that are readily carried along by the slightest breeze.

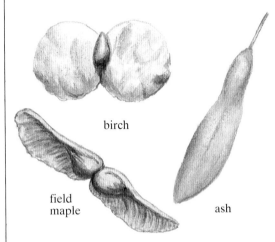

birch

field maple

ash

Willow and poplar seeds are also spread by wind. The fruits remain attached to the tree, but split to release numerous tiny seeds, each with a tuft of cottony hairs.

poplar

walnut

The seeds of some trees, for example hollies, European mountain ashes, hawthorns, cherries, blackthorn, and elders (*Sambucus* species) are enclosed in fleshy fruits. They are spread by animals. Birds feast on them during the winter months. The seeds inside have hard, woody coats that are damaged, but not digested, by the birds; they pass out in the droppings, ready to germinate in the spring.

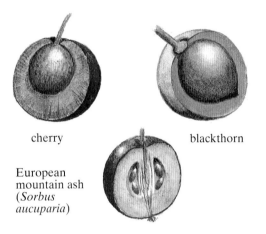

cherry

blackthorn

European mountain ash (*Sorbus aucuparia*)

Some trees such as hickories, oaks, beeches, hazels, and walnuts have large seeds called nuts. These are food for many animals such as squirrels, mice, and birds. Those that are eaten are digested and so do not have a chance to germinate, or grow. However, many birds and small animals make stores of nuts for winter. Some of the "larders" are forgotten and so are able to germinate in spring.

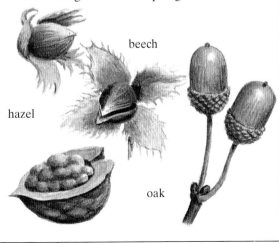

beech

hazel

oak

FRUITS OF THE FOREST

Many trees have fleshy fruits and berries, but they are mostly too sour for people to eat. However, crab apples, wild pears, and wild plums are all the ancestors of the sweet, juicy fruits that you eat today. Most wild fruit trees like open sites at the edge of woods or along fence lines. As many of them have pretty flowers in spring or red fruits in autumn, they are also planted as ornamental trees in gardens and parks. Apples, cherries, pears, plums, peaches, and apricots all belong to the rose family and are cultivated as fruit trees.

Rosy Fruits

Many of the fruit trees cultivated in orchards and gardens originally came from wild trees.

There are about 25 species of crab apple found in North America, Europe, and temperate Asia. Modern apples are descended from the crab apple (*Malus sylvestris*). Today there are about 6,000 varieties of apples.

Sweet cherries are all descended from the gean (*Prunus avium*), which grows wild in Europe, North Africa, and western Asia. It was cultivated in Egypt as early as 700 B.C., and there are now over 1,000 varieties. Cooking cherries have come from the sour cherry (*P. cerasus*), native to southeast Europe and southwest Asia.

Pears are descended from the common pear that is native to Europe and western Asia. Pears grow best in the warmer countries of the U.S. and Europe.

Plums originally came from western Asia. The plum tree (*Prunus domestica*) is probably a **hybrid** between blackthorn (*P. spinosa*) and cherry plum (*P. cerasifera*).

Peach (*Prunus persica*) and apricot (*P. armeniaca*) trees come from China. They grow well in the southern states of the U.S., and in the Mediterranean regions of Europe.

Old orchards

Fruit trees grow best in a warm climate, free from late frosts that kill the opening flowerbuds. So orchards are chiefly planted in sheltered parts of the U.S. and Europe. Older varieties of fruit trees were large and spreading – cherry trees would grow up to 100 feet tall. They were planted in widely spaced rows. Domestic animals, especially sheep, grazed in the orchards, keeping the grass short and fertilizing the ground with their droppings. Beehives were kept in the orchard to make sure that the flowers were pollinated.

Modern fruit farming

Today, fruit trees grown commercially are grafted onto dwarfing rootstocks, which makes them much smaller, only about 7 feet tall. They start to bear fruit when only three to four years old. It is much easier to pick the fruit from these small trees by hand and in large orchards they can even be harvested by machines.

As they do not have spreading branches, they can be planted closer together. Bees are still needed to pollinate the flowers, but other insects and diseases are killed with pesticide sprays. Some fruit growers plant their trees in huge polyethylene tunnels so that conditions can be controlled even more strictly. This has meant that much of the natural wildlife has been lost.

THE WOODLAND SOIL

Every autumn the woodland floor is covered with a layer of dead leaves. During the winter, rain, frost, and snow wet the fallen leaves and decay begins.

The leaf-litter (dead leaves) teems with life. Bacteria immediately begin to attack the dead leaves. Molds,

Earthworms are especially important. They drag leaves underground, and swallow soil and the particles of plant and animal remains that it contains. It is the action of large numbers of these earthworms that mixes and puts air into the soil.

All these organisms (living things)

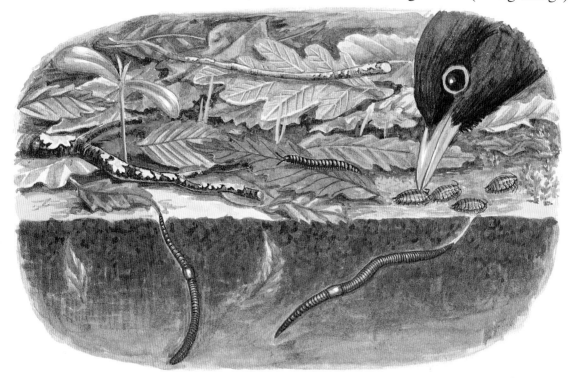

which are small kinds of fungi, also spread through the leaf-litter. They cannot photosynthesize, so they get all their food from the dead leaves. Tiny invertebrates (animals without backbones) – mites, springtails, fungus gnats, and woodlice – feed on the bacteria, molds, and leaf fragments.

reduce the leaf-litter to dark, rich compost. This releases and recycles nutrients that would otherwise remain locked up in the fallen leaves. These organisms form food for a chain of carnivorous (meat-eating) animals – beetles, spiders, moles, shrews, raccoons, and birds.

Brown forest soil

The fertile soil found in woodlands is called brown forest soil. Its depth and richness are two of the reasons that woodlands are cleared and turned into agricultural land. The deciduous woodlands of the northeast U.S. and eastern Asia and the oakwoods of the U.K. and west and central Europe all have this type of soil.

Brown forest soils lie upon rocks such as shales, fine sandstones, or basalts. Unlike most soil types, this soil does not form distinct layers. The action of the earthworms ensures that the top layer of compost is soon mixed into the deep loam beneath. Brown forest soils are well aerated, and hold enough moisture for trees to grow, without being waterlogged.

Ash forests

Another kind of soil, called rendzina, is found over chalk and limestone rocks. The dark brown or blackish topsoil is fertile but shallow and often contains lumps of chalk. Beech trees can grow on chalky or lime rendzinas because they have a naturally spreading, shallow root system.

Ash forests are found on rendzina soils formed on ancient limestone rocks. These trees are often small and slow-growing. They are far more lime-tolerant than most other trees and so can grow on these soils free from competition.

PIONEER TREES

Natural disasters such as fires, floods, land-slides, and gales can devastate woodlands, sometimes clearing quite large areas. If left alone, these areas, as well as those cleared deliberately by people, will eventually return to forest.

The trees that begin the process of recolonization and form the first stages of the new forest, the pioneers, are not always those that will finally dominate the forest canopy. Often the first trees have light, wind-blown seeds that are quick to germinate and grow. In wet places, these will be willows, poplars, and alders.

In the drier areas, birches such as silver birch (*Betula pendula*) soon spring up. Birches are short-lived trees, and are shaded out by taller trees. However, birchwoods persist on mountain slopes, light sandy soils, and at the edges of forests. Dwarf birches grow at the treeline on most mountain ranges and in the north outside the Arctic circle.

Lowland valleys
Lowland river valleys were once all woodlands. Today, most of this has been cleared, and crops or livestock are farmed in their place. Ribbons of moisture-loving trees still remain along the banks of these slow-moving rivers and streams. In Europe, white and crack willows (*Salix alba* and *S. fragilis*), white, gray, and black poplars (*Populus alba, P. canescens,* and *P. nigra*), as well as alders flourish. In North America, the eastern cottonwood (*Populus deltoides*), river birch (*Betula nigra*), and black willow (*Salix nigra*) are the trees of the riverbank.

Binding the soil

The tangled roots of riverside trees help to bind the banks and prevent erosion, the loss of soil, caused by the movement of the water. Even so, after heavy storms, rivers sometimes flood and burst their banks, leaving bare mud when the waters subside. These damp, open conditions are ideal for poplar and willow seeds which germinate and start to grow almost immediately. Their fast-growing roots soon stabilize the soft soil.

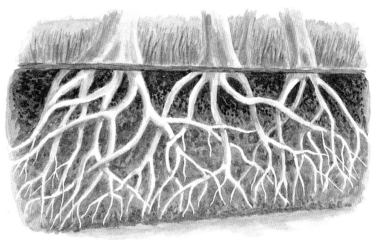

Trees of wet places

Within the woodland, there are low-lying areas where water collects and the ground becomes waterlogged. These wet, boggy conditions are usually near lowland rivers and lakes. Most woodland trees cannot grow in waterlogged soil because there is too little oxygen in the wet mud, and the roots cannot breathe. This means that there is a space in the forest canopy, allowing more light through so that trees such as alders, red or swamp maples, and aspens can grow.

The common alder (*Alnus glutinosa*) of the U.K., Europe, North Africa, and western Asia grows beside water to make a special kind of wet woodland, the alder carr. Alders and red maples are part of the natural succession, or change, of vegetation from the open water of a lake or marsh to woodland.

ONE TREE, MANY HOMES

Many woodland trees live to a great age. During their long life they develop a craggy bark full of crevices, gnarled roots, maybe a diseased branch that becomes hollow, and a crown of succulent buds, shoots, and leaves. The mature tree therefore provides a range of habitats or homes for numerous animals and smaller plants.

Similar groups of animals and plants are found at each level of the tree in temperate woods worldwide, but the species vary. Some insects with leaf-eating larvae can only live on particular trees. For instance, the oak hawkmoth caterpillars feed only on oak leaves. The lime hawkmoth larvae will, however, eat leaves of oak, alder, birch, and elm.

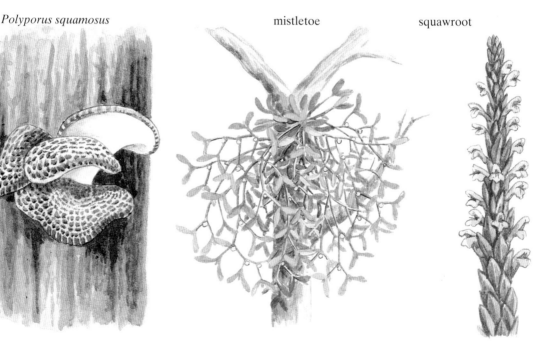

Polyporus squamosus   mistletoe   squawroot

Saprophytes and parasites

Plants that live on and obtain nutrients from dead plants such as fallen leaves or rotting logs are called **saprophytes**. Many fungi and molds live like this. Other plants penetrate the stem or roots of a living plant, and steal some of its nutrients. These are called **parasites**. Parasitic fungi include wood-rotting bracket fungus, which attacks elm, beech, and sycamore trees.

Flowering plants can be parasitic, too. Mistletoe (*Viscum album*) prefers to grow on branches of apple and poplar trees. It makes some of its food by photosynthesis, but takes mineral nutrients from its host's sap. Toothwort (*Lathraea squamaria*) grows on the roots of hazel and elms, and in North America its relative squawroot (*Conopholis americana*) is parasitic on oak roots.

THE DECIDUOUS TREE

Birds of prey nest in the crown.

Myriads of flying insects in leafy crown, often with leaf-eating caterpillars.

Birds (e.g. tits, finches) feed on the insects.

The golden oriole is a tree-canopy bird of Europe and western Asia.

Many birds feed on buds and shoots.

Moss grows even on twigs in damp, shady places.

Wood-rotting fungi enter through a wound.

Cushiony tufts of mosses and lichens grow.

Lichens

Bats live in hollow branches.

Wood-boring insects live beneath the bark. Insects and spiders live on the bark.

Insects live in the bark crevices.

Thick growth of mosses and liverwort thrive on damp base of tree trunk.

Many fungi grow in close association with tree roots.

Mosses grow among the roots in large clumps.

Mice, rabbits, and shrews live in burrows beneath roots.

THREATS TO WOODLANDS

Deciduous woodlands were one of the first kinds of vegetation to be affected by people. The mild climate, the deep, fertile soil, and the plentiful supply of streams and rivers made woodlands good places to settle. Felled trees provided building material and fuel for warmth and cooking. Yesterday's small villages are today's cities and spreading suburbs. Crops are planted on the deep soil, but its fertility is maintained by artificial fertilizers.

People are more aware now of the importance of woods, yet still they are being cleared for roads and houses, or even for new towns. Woodlands provide habitats for many animals. When the trees are cut down, the animals and plants that live on them go, too. The glades, clearings, and dense, shrubby thickets that are all part of the woodland environment are also lost. It means the loss of a place to live for possums, wild pigs, bears, deer, and foxes. These large animals suffer first because they need a large territory in which to forage.

Although smaller woodland creatures can adapt to living in parks and gardens, many are under threat and some have become extinct.

Bechstein's bat

When Britain and Europe were extensively covered by dense deciduous woodlands, Bechstein's bat was probably the commonest bat. As the forests dwindled, so too did the numbers of this bat. It is now so rare that little is known about its life-history and behavior. One of the reasons it is thought to have declined so drastically is because it roosts and breeds in old, hollow trees. These are only found in ancient woodlands; trees found in gardens, parks, and plantations are too young.

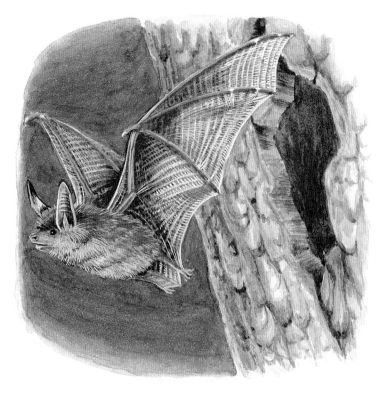

Wood duck

This duck lives and feeds in the deciduous woodlands of the northeast U.S. It nests in tree-holes in trees near open water or swamps. It was once very common, but when settlers cleared large areas of these woods in the nineteenth century, its habitat was lost. The ducks were also shot in great numbers, partly for sport and because they were good to eat, and partly for the splendid breeding plumage of the male duck, the drake. At the beginning of the twentieth century the duck was almost extinct, but fortunately conservation measures to protect the bird have saved it.

Mandarin duck

This northeast Asian duck is related to the North American wood duck and, like it, lives in deciduous woodlands. The drake also has very beautiful breeding plumage. It was once safe in the forests of the Manchu emperors in China. After they were deposed in 1911, the forests were cleared. The number of these ducks in China is not known, although it is thought to be rare. Fortunately, it also occurs in Japan, and it is in no danger of **extinction** (dying out) – especially as birds that escaped from wildfowl collections in Britain are now breeding well and increasing in numbers in southern England.

DISAPPEARING WOODLANDS

There is a huge demand all over the world for wood, and much of this is for wood pulp that is made into paper. Wood pulp is chiefly produced from conifers, which are often specially grown for this purpose in plantations. These plantations frequently replace deciduous woodlands. Nearly all broad-leaved trees are slow-growing compared with conifers. This means that it is a long time – as much as 100 years – before trees such as oaks are ready to be felled.

As the conifer trees grow, their evergreen canopy becomes thick, letting very little light through to the ground. Conifer needles do not rot in the same way as leaves; they decay very slowly, making an infertile, acid leaf-litter. Many organisms that break down decaying matter, including earthworms, cannot live in these conditions, so many woodland plants and animals disappear. The soil becomes less fertile as nutrients removed by the growing trees remain locked up in the leaf-litter.

Many trees are also damaged or killed when harmful insects and diseases are introduced into a country. This can happen when diseased timber is imported or when new species of tree are introduced.

Dutch elm disease
Neither dutch elm disease nor the bark beetle that spreads it was found in the U.S. until they were accidentally introduced on infected timber during the 1930s. The disease spread quickly across North America, particularly affecting and killing the American elm. Although the early outbreak in Europe died down naturally, the disease was brought back from the U.S. in the 1960s, again on infected timber. This started the epidemic that for about the next 10 years steadily killed virtually all the English elm (*Ulmus procera*) of lowland Britain.

Trees and the atmosphere

There are many chemicals locked up in a forest tree. When leaves fall, or an old tree rots, these substances are released by the activity of various organisms and can be reabsorbed by living trees or enter an animal food chain. Use and reuse of these chemicals is called a nutrient cycle.

When forests are cleared on a large scale this balance is upset. Wood and fossil fuels such as coal and oil release vast amounts of carbon dioxide into the air when burned. If felled forests are not replaced by new trees, there is nothing to use up and remove carbon dioxide from the atmosphere. As carbon dioxide builds up in the atmosphere, it traps the heat of the sun and increases the greenhouse effect. This results in the warming of land and sea, which may cause great problems in the future.

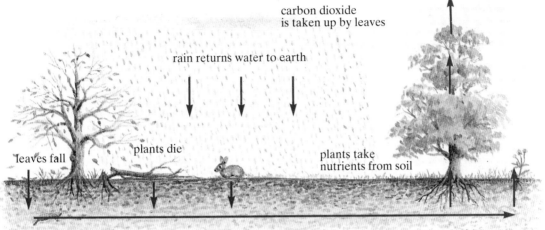

plants expel moisture into the atmosphere

carbon dioxide is taken up by leaves

rain returns water to earth

leaves fall

plants die

plants take nutrients from soil

organic matter breaks down into soil

Chestnut blight

In China, the fungus that causes chestnut blight does not seriously affect the Chinese chestnut (*Castanea mollissima*), as it has a natural resistance to it. However, in 1904 infected wood was imported into the U.S. The American chestnut (*C. dentata*) then made up about 40 percent of parts of the eastern woods. It had never before been exposed to chestnut blight fungus. Within 20 or 30 years, the blight had killed almost all the American chestnuts.

TIMBER

Wood is a very valuable commodity. More than 100 billion cubic feet are consumed annually, but only about 17 percent of this comes from temperate woodlands. The timber of many broad-leaved trees is hard, strong, and very long lasting. Broad-leaved trees are often called the hardwoods. The felled hardwood trunk is sawn into planks while "green," or still full of sap. The planks are then stored and seasoned, to allow the sap to dry out.

Skilled carpenters still work with hardwood timbers to make beautiful but expensive furniture. In Europe and Asia, common walnut (*Juglans regia*) is used, while in North America black walnut (*J. nigra*), and in Japan, Japanese walnut (*J. ailantifolia*) are the most common.

Oaks also provide top-grade timber. It is so strong that its use in building houses only decreased when steel girders became available. Ships were once built of oak. It is still made into furniture, and has many other uses. In the U.K. and Europe, pedunculate oak is the most important. White oak is one of the best timber oaks in the U.S., and in northeast Asia and Japan, *Quercus mongolica* is the best.

Wood for furniture
Beeches are also used for furniture-making. Many furniture industries have developed close to their source of supply, and the chair-makers of the Chilterns in the U.K. are a good example of this. Beech is used for the framework of many armchairs and sofas produced in the U.S. and Europe today.

Less well-known timbers are also important in their native countries. Keaki (*Zelkova serrata*) is an important timber tree in Japan, where it is used to build boats as well as furniture. Various species of southern beech are used for furniture in New Zealand and Chile.

Specialist Woods

Other trees have wood best suited to more specialized uses. Many of these have been superseded by metals and modern materials such as nylon, plastics, and fiberglass, but many people still prefer wood.

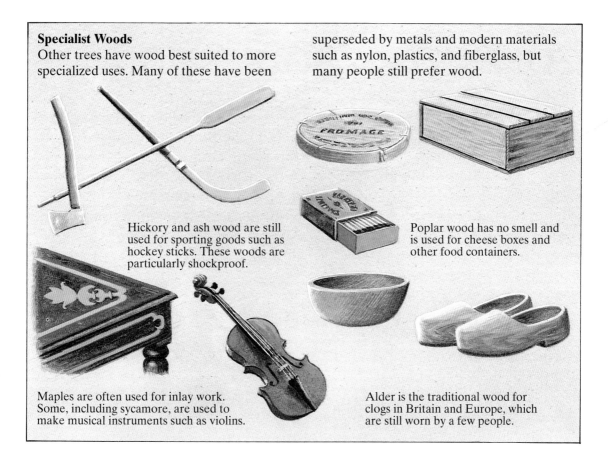

Hickory and ash wood are still used for sporting goods such as hockey sticks. These woods are particularly shockproof.

Poplar wood has no smell and is used for cheese boxes and other food containers.

Maples are often used for inlay work. Some, including sycamore, are used to make musical instruments such as violins.

Alder is the traditional wood for clogs in Britain and Europe, which are still worn by a few people.

Poplar plantations

About 200 years ago, the eastern cottonwood was introduced to Europe from North America. It crossed, or interbred, with the European black poplar to form a hybrid tree. Foresters breed many different strains or cultivars that are grown in plantations. In the right conditions, they grow as fast, if not faster than, conifers. These hybrid poplars can be felled when only 30 years old. The pale wood is ideal for wood pulp and match-making, and poplar poles are used in eastern Europe for building houses.

COPPICED WOODLAND

If broad-leaved trees are felled, new shoots spring up around the stump. These grow quickly to make a clump of more or less evenly sized poles. When these are cut to the ground, another crop grows in their place. This is known as **coppicing**. A practice common in Europe, coppicing can be repeated many times until the old tree base, called a stool, needs replacing.

Coppicing woodlands therefore provides a constant supply of small poles, which have a great variety of uses. The area under coppice is divided into plots, each of which is cut in turn. Willows can be cut every three years, but oak and alder are cut every 21 to 25 years. So to ensure a harvest each year, the number of plots required equals the number of years it takes for the shoots to grow.

The environment is also greatly improved by coppicing. The soil in coppiced woodland is a fertile loam, which improves with the age of the coppice. Coppices provide a range of smaller habitats. Recently cut plots are open and grassy. Plots nearing harvest are densely twiggy, with a leafy canopy in summer. They are good sites for woodland flowers, and for butterflies, moths, and small woodland birds such as warblers.

Osiers

Osiers such as purple willow (*Salix purpurea*) are cultivated for their long, thin twigs used for making baskets. Basketry was a widespread, commonplace rural industry, supplying men and women with all kinds of hard-wearing baskets and crates. When cardboard and plastic containers became cheap and readily available, the once-flourishing industry became little more than a quaint craft.

Benefits of Coppicing

Coppicing was once popular, but it declined as demand fell and conifer plantations were developed. However, there are now signs that people are once more realizing the benefits of coppicing.

■ There is still a great demand for wood for fuel, particularly with the increase in popularity of wood-burning stoves.

■ To replace conifer plantations with more natural deciduous woodlands.

■ Food "mountains" in the countries of the European Community (EC) have meant that farmers are being asked to produce less grain and use the land in other ways.

■ People are now eager to revive old rural skills. Many people believe that modern materials are not always better than the traditional ones.

Uses of coppice poles

Oak, which was once used to make charcoal for the iron industry, and the bark used to tan hides, is now used for fuel and fencing.

Hazel is used in Europe to make sticks for farmers and gardeners, and thatching spars.

Willow is used in basketry.

Sweet chestnut is used to make fine furniture.

Hornbeam (*Carpinus betulus*) makes excellent firewood.

Birch makes special garden brooms called besoms.

Sycamore maple is used to make bowls, kitchen utensils, and fencing.

Alder is used to make clogs, wooden ornaments, and underwater piling.

Ash is used to make ladders, walking sticks, and tool handles.

Linden is used to make small boxes and beehive frames.

Elm is used to make clapboard and kitchen chairs.

Black locust makes poles for vineyards.

41

OTHER WOODLAND PRODUCTS

oodland trees not only provide timber, they also supply people with foods. For example, nuts are tasty and very nutritious. They are the large seeds of various trees, and are rich in oils and proteins. They also keep well throughout the winter, protected inside hard, woody shells. Chestnuts were even ground into flour and made into bread by villagers in southern France. Nuts are still an important source of protein, especially for vegetarians, who do not eat meat.

Shiitake, an edible fungus eaten in Japan, grows on the wood of the golden chestnut (*Chrysolepis cuspidata*). To cultivate this fungus commercially, piles of chestnut logs are stacked up. They are injected with shiitake spores, and the resulting fruiting bodies, or mushrooms, of the fungus are harvested and eaten.

Maple syrup

The North American Indians obtained sugar from the sap of the sugar maple by drying it on hot stones. The early settlers improved upon this process, and it became a good source of sugar in the nineteenth century, with more flavor than cane sugar. Today the sap tapped from the sugar maple is made into maple syrup, which is delicious on waffles, pancakes, and ice cream. Up to 24 gallons of sap can be drained, or tapped, from a large tree each spring, apparently without harming the tree in any way. The sap is then concentrated by boiling, to yield only about 2.5 quarts of syrup.

Medicines

Many medicines are made from woodland trees. The bark of twigs of white, crack, and purple willows contain the chemical salicin. Today, this is prepared synthetically by drug companies and sold as aspirin, but before this was possible, willow bark was used to treat headaches, fevers, and rheumatic pains.

The slippery elm (*Ulmus rubra*) grows in North America. Beneath its thick bark is a white, gummy layer that can be made into a soothing drink for upset stomachs.

Tea made from dried lime flowers is popular in continental Europe. It counteracts the effects of eating and drinking too much. In North America, basswood flowers are used.

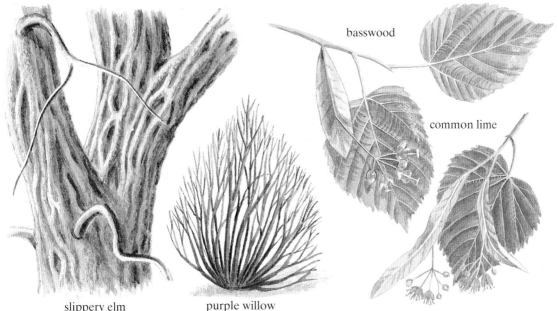

basswood

common lime

slippery elm

purple willow

Cork

Cork is the best material for heat, sound, and moisture insulation. It is obtained from the bark of the cork oak (*Quercus suber*), a small evergreen tree that grows in woods in the Mediterranean region. It is also cultivated in other warm countries such as the southern states of the U.S. Its thick, corky bark can grow up to 3 inches or more. To harvest the cork, the bark is stripped from the tree trunk every 10 years. Most cork comes from Portugal and Spain, where some oaks have been periodically stripped of their bark for 500 years or more.

GLOSSARY

BARK – The tough outer layer of tree trunks and branches.

BIOME – A zone of vegetation and the animals that live in it.

CAMBIUM – The growing layer that makes the trunk and branches a little thicker each year.

CANOPY – The top layer of leaves, which in woodlands is made up of the crowns of trees.

CARPEL – The female part of a flower made up of a style, a stigma, and an ovary containing the ovule.

CHLOROPHYLL – The green pigment in plants that absorbs energy from sunlight to make food by photosynthesis.

COPPICING – The practice of cutting the trunk of a tree close to the ground so that it sprouts several fast-growing shoots.

CROWN – The upper part of a tree, made up of its branches, twigs, and leaves.

CULTIVAR – A specially bred, cultivated variety of plant.

CUTICLE – The waterproof, waxy skin of leaves, young shoots, and flowers.

ECOSYSTEM – Communities of animals and plants in their nonliving environment.

EXTINCTION – The complete disappearance and loss of a species.

FERTILIZE – When a male pollen cell joins with a female ovule.

FRUIT – The part of a flower that contains and protects the developing seeds.

HEARTWOOD – The nonliving, but very strong, wood that makes up the central core of a tree trunk.

HYBRID – A plant or animal that results from two different species crossbreeding.

OVULE – The female cell that grows into a seed after fertilization.

PARASITE – A plant or animal that obtains its food from the living body of another plant or animal.

PHLOEM – The narrow layer beneath the bark that carries sugars from the leaves to other parts of the tree.

PHOTOSYNTHESIS – The process in green plants that uses the energy in sunlight to turn carbon dioxide gas and water vapor into sugars, releasing oxygen.

POLLEN – The powdery grains that are shed by the stamens and contain the male sex cells.

POLLINATION – This is when the male pollen lands on a specially receptive part of the carpel.

SAP – The watery juice in living plant cells.

SAPROPHYTE – A plant that obtains its nutrients from dead plant material.

SAPWOOD – The living layer of wood through which water taken up by the roots passes up the tree.

STAMEN – The male part of a flower.

STOMATA (singular stoma) – Tiny holes in the surface of a leaf through which gases and water vapor can pass.

SUCKERS – Shoots that grow up from the roots of a tree, often some distance away from the main trunk.

TRUNK – The large, woody stem of a tree.

UNDERSTORY – The shrubs and small trees that grow among the taller woodland trees.

XYLEM – Woody cells that conduct water in the sapwood.

ZONE – A large area of natural vegetation.

FURTHER READING

For children
Forests by Donna Bailey; Steck-Vaughn, 1989.
The Trees of North America by Alan Mitchell; Facts on File, 1987.

For adults
Field Guide to North American Trees: Eastern Edition by Audubon Society Staff and Elbert L. Little; Knopf, 1980.
Field Guide to North American Trees: Western Edition by Audubon Society Staff and Elbert L. Little; Knopf, 1980.
The Audubon Society Book of Trees (Audubon Society Series); Abrams, 1981.

TREES IN THIS BOOK

American chestnut (*Castanea dentata*)
American elm (*Ulmus americana*)
American sycamore (*Platanus occidentalis*)
Antarctic beech (*Nothofagus antarctica*)
Apricot (*Prunus armeniaca*)
Aspens (*Populus* species)
Basswood (*Tilia americana*)
Bitternut (*Carya cordiformis*)
Black locust (*Robinia pseudacacia*)
Black oak (*Quercus velutina*)
Black poplar (*Populus nigra*)
Blackthorn (*Prunus spinosa*)
Black walnut (*Juglans nigra*)
Black willow (*Salix nigra*)
Cherry plum (*Prunus cerasifera*)
Chinese chestnut (*Castanea mollissima*)
Coigue (*Nothofagus dombeyi*)
Common alder (*Alnus glutinosa*)
Common pear (*Pyrus communis*)
Common walnut (*Juglans regia*)
Cork oak (*Quercus suber*)
Crab apple (*Malus sylvestris*)
Crack willow (*Salix fragilis*)
Eastern cottonwood (*Populus deltoides*)
Elder (*Sambucus* species)
English elm (*Ulmus procera*)
English or pedunculate oak (*Quercus robur*)
European ash (*Fraxinus excelsior*)
European beech (*Fagus sylvatica*)
European mountain ash (*Sorbus aucuparia*)
Gean (*Prunus avium*)
Golden chestnut (*Chrysolepis cuspidata*)
Gray poplar (*Populus canescens*)
Hawthorn (*Crataegus* species)
Hazel (*Corylus avellana*)
Hickory (*Carya* species)
Holly (*Ilex aquilifolium*)
Hornbeam (*Carpinus betulus*)
Horse chestnut (*Aesculus hippocastanum*)
Japanese cherry (*Prunus serratula*)
Japanese elm (*Ulmus japonica*)
Japanese magnolia (*Magnolia hypoleuca*)
Japanese maple (*Acer japonicum*)
Japanese walnut (*Juglans ailantifolia*)

Katsura tree (*Cercidiphyllum japonicum*)
Keaki (*Zelkova serrata*)
Kowhai (*Sophora tetraptera*)
Large-leaved linden (*Tilia platyphyllos*)
Laurel (*Laurus nobilis*)
Lenga (*Nothofagus pumilio*)
Mockernut (*Carya tomentosa*)
New Zealand red beech (*Nothofagus fusca*)
Oriental beech (*Fagus orientalis*)
Oval-leaved beech (*Nothofagus betuloides*)
Pagoda tree (*Sophora japonica*)
Peach (*Prúnus persica*)
Plane (*Platanus* species)
Plum (*Prunus domestica*)
Purple willow (*Salix purpurea*)
Quercus mongolica
Raoul (*Nothofagus procera*)
Red maple (*Acer rubrum*)
Red oak (*Quercus rubra*)
River birch (*Betula nigra*)
Roblé (*Nothofagus obliqua*)
Scarlet oak (*Quercus coccinea*)
Silver birch (*Betula pendula*)
Silver maple (*Acer saccharinum*)
Slippery elm (*Ulmus rubra*)
Sour cherry (*Prunus cerasus*)
Stag's horn sumach (*Rhus typhina*)
Sugar maple (*Acer saccharum*)
Sweet chestnut (*Castanea sativa*)
Sweetgum (*Liquidambar styraciflua*)
Sycamore (*Acer pseudoplatanus*)
Tasmanian beech (*Nothofagus cunninghamii*)
Tree of heaven (*Ailanthus altissima*)
Tulip tree (*Liriodendron tulipifera*)
Western balsam poplar (*Populus trichocarpa*)
White ash (*Fraxinus americana*)
White hickory (*Carya alba*)
White mulberry (*Morus alba*)
White poplar (*Populus alba*)
White willow (*Salix alba*)
Willow oak (*Quercus phellos*)
Wing-nut (*Pterocarya* species)
Yellow birch (*Betula lutea*)
Yoshino cherry (*Prunus yedoensis*)

INDEX